Warm Up your Winter

Holiday
& Hot Chocolate
Cider Recipes

Laura Powell

• FROM REALMOMKITCHEN.COM •

Front Table Books
An Imprint of Cedar Fort, Inc.
Springville, Utah

ISBN: 978-1-4621-1204-3

Published by Front Table Books, an imprint of Cedar Fort, Inc.
2373 W. 700 S., Springville, UT 84663
Distributed by Cedar Fort, Inc., www.cedarfort.com

Library of Congress Cataloging-in-Publication Data

Powell, Laura (Laura Whittemore), 1974-
Warm up your winter : holiday hot chocolate and cider recipes / Laura Powell.
    pages cm
 ISBN 978-1-4621-1204-3
 1. Chocolate drinks. 2. Cider. I. Title.
  TX817.C4P69 2013
  641.3'374--dc23
                              2013017397

Cover and page design by Erica Dixon
Cover design © 2013 Lyle Mortimer
Edited by Casey J. Winters

Printed in the United States of America

10 9 8 7 6 5 4 3 2 1

Thanks to my family for all of their help and support.

Thanks to my mom and husband for being my at-home editors.

And special thanks to my husband for editing my photos so they could look their best!

· Contents ·

Nutella Hot Chocolate

This decadent hazelnut-flavored hot chocolate comes together quickly with only two ingredients. Whole milk makes it nice and rich, but feel free to use 2%, 1%, or skim milk in its place.

4 cups whole milk

½ cup Nutella or similar chocolate hazelnut spread

mini marshmallows or whipped cream, optional

1. **In a medium saucepan** over medium-low heat, whisk together milk and Nutella until the Nutella is dissolved and milk is warm.

2. **Serve in mugs** and top with marshmallows or whipped cream.

Note: This can be made ahead of time, cooled, and stored in the fridge. Reheat on the stove or in the microwave in individual mugs. To microwave, reheat each cup for about 1 minute.

Makes 4 (8-oz.) servings

Frozen Hot Chocolate

Not up for a hot chocolate?
Then give this chilly frozen version a try.

½ cup semisweet or milk chocolate chips, or 4 oz. chocolate

2 tsp. hot cocoa mix

1½ Tbsp. sugar

1½ cups milk, divided

3 cups ice cubes

sweetened whipped cream

chocolate shavings, optional

1. Chop chocolate into small pieces and melt in microwave at 10-second intervals until melted.

2. Add hot cocoa mix and sugar to the melted chocolate. Mix until thoroughly blended.

3. Slowly add ½ cup milk, stirring until smooth. Set aside and allow to cool to room temperature.

4. In blender, place the remaining 1 cup milk, cooled chocolate mixture, and ice cubes. Blend on high speed until smooth and the consistency of a frozen daiquiri.

5. Pour in mugs and top with whipped cream and optional chocolate shavings.

Makes 4 (8-oz.) servings

Hot Vanilla

If chocolate isn't what you are looking for, then try this version of a hot vanilla drink topped with chocolate whipped cream.

½ cup whipping cream

1 Tbsp. chocolate syrup

dash of cinnamon

6 cups milk

¼ cup sugar

2 Tbsp. vanilla extract

additional chocolate syrup for garnish, optional

1. In a medium bowl, whip whipping cream until frothy. Add chocolate syrup and cinnamon. Continue to whip the mixture until firm peaks form. Set aside.

2. In a saucepan, combine milk and sugar. Cook until warm and sugar is dissolved. Remove from heat and mix in vanilla. Pour into mugs and top each mug with a dollop of the prepared chocolate cream and a drizzle of chocolate syrup, if desired.

Makes 6 (8-oz.) servings

Best Ever Hot Cocoa Mix

This recipe uses Dutch-processed cocoa powder. "Dutch processing" is simply a way of processing the cocoa that gives it a mild yet more chocolaty flavor. Regular cocoa powder can be substituted if needed.

3 cups nonfat dry milk

1½ cups white chocolate chips

2 cups (8 oz.) confectioners' sugar

1½ cups Dutch-processed cocoa

¼ tsp. salt

1. Place the dry milk and white chocolate chips into a food processor or high-powered blender. Process these ingredients in the food processor or blender until it becomes a powder.

2. Add the powder to a large bowl and add the remaining ingredients. Whisk together until well blended with no clumps. (The white chocolate/dry milk mixture likes to clump together.)

3. Store in an airtight container. Will store for 3 months.

To make hot cocoa, add ⅓ cup of this mixture into 1 cup of hot milk and stir until well combined and the mixture has dissolved.

Note: This recipe can also be made with other types of chocolate chips for different flavors.

Makes 20 (8-oz.) servings

Classic Hot Cocoa

This hot chocolate is better than anything you can get in a mix. It is rich, creamy, and full of chocolate flavor. The whole milk is what helps make it so yummy. You could use 2%, 1%, or skim if you want to, but going for the whole milk is worth it!

½ cup sugar

$^1/_3$ cup unsweetened cocoa powder

$^1/_8$ tsp. salt

$^1/_3$ cup half-and-half

4 cups whole milk

whipped cream or mini marshmallows

1. In a medium saucepan, whisk together sugar, cocoa, and salt until blended. Then whisk in half-and-half.

2. Cook over medium heat, stirring constantly, until mixture comes to a boil.

3. Simmer 1–2 minutes, stirring constantly.

4. Add milk. Stirring constantly, heat until warm. DO NOT BOIL.

5. Remove cocoa from heat and whisk or beat until frothy. Pour into mugs and top with whipped cream or mini marshmallows.

Makes 4 (8-oz.) servings

Variations

Use the recipe on the previous page, with the following changes:

Skinny Cocoa: Eliminate sugar. Combine cocoa, salt, and ½ cup skim milk instead of half-and-half; use 4 cups skim milk or reconstituted non-fat dry milk instead of whole milk. Proceed with directions. When removing from heat, stir in enough sugar substitute with sweetening equivalent to ½ cup sugar.

Butterscotch Cocoa: Replace sugar with ¼ cup brown sugar. Before adding milk, stir in 1 cup butterscotch baking chips. (Replacing the sugar with brown sugar also goes well with Harvest Spice or Peanut Butter Cocoa variations.)

Canadian Cocoa: Add ½–1 tsp. maple extract after removing from heat.

Cocoa au Lait: Serve with a scoop of softened vanilla ice cream on top of each cup.

Eggnog Cocoa: Eliminate sugar, substitute ⅓ cup milk for half-and-half, and substitute 4 cups prepared eggnog for milk. Sprinkle with nutmeg if desired.

Harvest Spice Cocoa: Add 1–3 tsp. pumpkin pie spice to cocoa powder.

Mexican Cocoa: Add ½–1 tsp. ground cinnamon to cocoa powder.

Orange Cocoa: Add ½ tsp. orange extract when removing from heat.

Peanut Butter or Nutella Cocoa: Replace sugar with ⅓ cup brown sugar. Add ¼–½ cup creamy peanut butter or Nutella before adding milk; stir until smooth and then add milk.

Peppermint Cocoa: Add ½ tsp. mint and crushed peppermint candies when adding milk and stir until candies are dissolved.

Almond Cocoa: Add ½ tsp. almond extract when adding milk.

Sweet Slow Cooker Hot Chocolate

This recipe calls for a can of sweetened condensed milk, which gives it some extra sweetness. The thing I love about this recipe is that if you give the hot chocolate a good whisking after it's finished, you can get a little froth top on it. Mmmmmmm.

1½ cups heavy cream

1 (14-oz.) can sweetened condensed milk

2 cups milk chocolate chips

6 cups milk

1 tsp. vanilla extract

1. Add all the ingredients to your slow cooker and stir until the condensed milk is well blended into the mixture.

2. Cover and cook on low for 2 hours, whisking it every 30 minutes.

3. Once the 2 hours are up, give it a final whisk and serve.

Makes 12 (1-cup) servings

Homemade Hot Cocoa Mix

When I was a young girl, I remember making homemade hot cocoa mix and placing it in mugs to give my friends as a Christmas gift. The recipe I made was similar to this recipe, but I think this recipe is even better. I think the instant chocolate pudding mix is the secret! Mix this up to keep on hand for a quick cup of hot cocoa. You could also surprise a friend with a simple gift.

4 cups nonfat dry milk powder

1½ cups sugar

1 cup nondairy powdered coffee creamer

²/₃ cup unsweetened cocoa powder

1 (4-oz.) pkg. instant chocolate pudding

1. Place all of the above ingredients together in a large bowl.

2. Whisk together until well combined.

3. Store in an airtight container.

To prepare a cup of hot cocoa, add ¼ or ¹/₃ cup of mix (I like ¹/₃ cup) to 8 ounces of hot water. Stir until blended.

Note: Different flavors of nondairy powdered coffee creamers can be used to make a gourmet version.

Makes 22 servings using ¹/₃-cup mix or 30 servings using ¼-cup mix

Rich and Decadent Hot Chocolate

Hot chocolate is usually made with actual chocolate, whereas hot cocoa is made with cocoa powder. This version is extremely chocolaty. I would say it is the espresso equivalent for the hot chocolate family. This is seriously just like chocolate in drinkable form. If it is too rich for you, then add some milk to reduce the intensity. I loved it and think it could even be served as a dessert.

1 (12-oz.) can evaporated milk

4 oz. semisweet chocolate or ½ cup semisweet chocolate chips

¼ cup sugar

¼ tsp. salt

1 tsp. vanilla extract

1. **In a small saucepan,** whisk together milk, chocolate, sugar, and salt over medium-low heat until the chocolate is completely melted and everything is blended together.

2. **Stir in vanilla.** Cover and cook on low heat for 7–8 minutes, stirring occasionally.

3. **Turn the heat off** and let the hot cocoa sit (still covered) for 5 minutes before serving. Give it a whisk and serve immediately.

Makes 6 (⅓-cup) servings

Hot Caramel Apple Cider

Hot apple cider is always delicious, but the addition of caramel makes it extra special. It's just like drinking a caramel apple!

8 cups or ½ gallon apple cider

¼ cup brown sugar

¼ cup caramel ice cream topping

whipped cream, optional

extra caramel ice cream topping, optional

1. In a large saucepan, combine cider, sugar, and caramel topping.

2. Cook over medium-low heat until simmering, stirring frequently. Simmer until heated and well blended.

3. Serve in mugs. Pipe whipping cream on top and drizzle with additional caramel topping if desired.

Makes 8 (8-oz.) servings

Hot Apple Cider

This recipe is your basic hot cider with some spices added for extra flavor. I really love this combination. It's also quick to make; no need to simmer all day. You'll be warming up in no time as you sip on this.

6 cups apple cider

¼ cup real maple syrup

6 whole cloves

1 orange, cut into quarters

2 cinnamon sticks

1 lemon, cut into fourths

6 whole allspice berries

1. In a large saucepan, combine the apple cider with the maple syrup.

2. Pierce the whole cloves into one of the orange quarters through the peel. Then add cinnamon sticks along with the lemon and orange pieces to the cider.

3. In a small piece of cheesecloth, add the allspice berries. Place in the cider.

4. Heat cider over medium heat for 10 minutes, stirring occasionally.

5. Using a slotted spoon, remove the cinnamon sticks, lemon, orange pieces, and the allspice berries in the cheesecloth. Serve cider in mugs.

Makes 6 (1-cup) servings

Hot Mulled Cider

This classic mulled cider recipe can be prepared in a slow cooker and left for hours, or on the stove top for quick preparation.

1 gallon apple cider

3 cinnamon sticks

1 Tbsp. whole cloves

1 tsp. whole allspice

rind of ½ an orange

For slow cooker method: Pour apple cider into slow cooker. Add the cinnamon sticks to the cider. In a square of cheesecloth, place cloves, allspice, and orange rind and then tie closed and place into cider. Cook on high for 2 hours. Remove cheesecloth bundle and cinnamon sticks. Ladle cider into mugs.

For stovetop method: Pour apple cider into a large pot. Add the cinnamon sticks to the cider. In a square of cheesecloth, place cloves, allspice, and orange rind and then tie closed and place into cider. Place pot on stove over medium heat until the cider just starts to boil. Reduce to simmer and cook for 15 minutes. Stir occasionally. Remove cheesecloth bundle and cinnamon sticks. Ladle cider into mugs.

Makes 16 (1-cup) servings

Individual Hot Caramel Apple Drink

This drink is perfect for when you are only serving one.

1 packet dry apple cider mix, or 1 cup apple cider or apple juice

1–2 tsp. cinnamon caramel apple dip**

additional cinnamon caramel dip for drizzling

whipped cream

1. **Dissolve cider mix** in 8 ounces of very hot water, or heat apple cider until warm. Stir in cinnamon caramel dip. Stir until well blended. Give the cider a minute or two to cool.

2. **While cooling,** put a spoonful of cinnamon caramel dip in a zip-top sandwich bag. Snip off a small corner of the bag.

3. **Top cider with whipped cream** and use the bag with caramel to pipe a drizzle of the cinnamon caramel dip over the whipped cream.

**Note: Regular caramel apple dip or caramel ice cream topping may also be used.*

Makes 1 (8-oz.) serving

Salted Caramel Hot Chocolate

This recipe combines two well known flavors—chocolate and caramel!

1 cup whipping cream

8 (.53-oz. each) squares dark chocolate and caramel (like Ghirardelli)

¼ cup brown sugar

4 cups of milk

¼ tsp. salt

whipped cream

caramel ice cream topping

1. **In a saucepan,** cook whipping cream, chocolate and caramel squares, and brown sugar over medium-low heat until chocolate is melted and sugar is dissolved.

2. **Add milk and salt** and whisk together. Bring heat up and heat until desired temperature is reached.

3. **Ladle into mugs** and top with whipped cream followed by a good drizzle of caramel ice cream topping.

Note: The flavor of this hot chocolate can be changed by using different chocolate squares, such as dark chocolate and raspberry or dark chocolate and mint.

Makes 5 (8-oz.) servings

Hot Chocolate Truffles

Hot chocolate made from a truffle. Sounds fabulous, huh?
It is so delicious. They are simple to make and would be a great gift.
Get a mug, fill it with some marshmallows and these
truffles, and you are all set!

1 (12-oz.) pkg. dark chocolate chips or semisweet chocolate chips

1 cup heavy cream

1 Tbsp. sugar

$^1/_8$ tsp. salt

2 packets hot cocoa mix, or 20 mini peppermint candy canes, crushed**

1. **Place all ingredients,** except cocoa mix/crushed candy canes, in a double boiler*** and stir until chocolate is melted and all the ingredients are well combined. Whisk until smooth.

2. **Allow the mixture** to cool until it is no longer hot—can be slightly warm. Cover the bowl with plastic wrap and refrigerate for about 2–3 hours until firm.

3. **Using a cookie scoop,** scoop the chocolate mixture (approx. 1-inch scoops) and drop each scoop into a bowl filled with the cocoa mix or crushed peppermint candy canes. Roll each ball into the mixture to coat. Immediately place each ball onto a square of plastic wrap. Wrap up each ball with plastic wrap to seal. Place balls in a freezer bag and freeze until ready to use.

Makes 20-22 balls

To make the hot chocolate: Place 1 cup of milk into a microwave-safe mug. Carefully drop two unwrapped hot chocolate truffles into the milk and microwave for about 1 minute. Stir, and microwave for 30–60 more seconds, until the truffles dissolve into the milk. Serve warm!

** To crush candy canes, place the wrapped candy canes on a hard surface and pound with a rolling pin. A small amount of candy may sneak out of the wrappers, but it mostly stays in the wrappers. Open wrappers and place candy in a bowl. See below for some candy cane variations.

*** This can be made in the microwave instead of a double boiler. In a microwave-safe bowl, combine all of the ingredients. Microwave for 30 seconds and stir. Then microwave in 20-second intervals until well combined and smooth. Stir well after each interval. Be careful not to overheat or the chocolate will seize. Follow remainder of the recipe from step 2.

Variations:

Strawberry candy canes: Chocolate-Dipped Strawberry Hot Chocolate

Cherry candy canes: Cherry Cordial Hot Chocolate

Orange candy canes: Orange Stick Hot Chocolate

Raspberry candy canes: Raspberry Truffle Hot Chocolate

Pumpkin Pie White Hot Chocolate

If you love pumpkin pie, then this hot chocolate is for you.
It's like you're drinking pumpkin pie.

1 cup white chocolate chips

1 cup whipping cream

4 cups milk

½ tsp. vanilla

½ cup canned pumpkin puree

½ tsp. pumpkin spice, plus additional for garnish

pinch of ground cloves

pinch of salt

whipped cream

1. **In a saucepan,** cook white chocolate and whipping cream over medium-low heat until chocolate is melted.

2. **Add milk,** vanilla, pumpkin puree, ½ teaspoon pumpkin pie spice, ground cloves, and salt. Whisk together. Bring heat up and heat until desired temperature is reached.

3. **Ladle into mugs** and top with whipped cream followed by a dash of pumpkin pie spice.

Note: Milk chocolate or semisweet chocolate may be used in place of the white chocolate.

Makes 5 (8-oz.) servings

Marshmallow Whipped Cream

My favorite way to top my hot cocoa or hot chocolate is with whipped cream. This recipe is where two favorite hot cocoa toppers meet to make one fabulous way to finish off a steamy hot cup of cocoa. I like to let the marshmallows sit in the cream for a bit before using it. Then the marshmallows get all puffy and soft.

1 cup whipping cream

1–2 Tbsp. powdered sugar

dash of vanilla

1–2 cups mini marshmallows

1. In a bowl, whip cream until firm.

2. Blend in sugar and vanilla.

3. Fold in marshmallows. Use immediately to top cups of hot cocoa if desired. Or place in the fridge for a few hours, and the marshmallows will puff up and soften.

Peppermint Whipped Cream

My favorite way to top my hot cocoa or hot chocolate is with whipped cream. This recipe gives the whipped cream a twist of peppermint by mixing in crushed candy canes. Also, I love its beautiful pink color.

6 red-and-white peppermint candy canes or 24 red and white mini peppermint candy canes

2 cups whipping cream

1. Unwrap candy canes and place them in a blender or food processor.

2. Process candy canes until they are a fairly fine powder.

3. In another bowl, whip cream until firm. No need to add sugar; the candy canes will sweeten it.

4. Fold the candy cane powder into the cream. Use immediately to top your cocoa if you like little pieces of crunchy candy cane in it. Or place in the refrigerator for 2 hours and allow the candy canes to completely dissolve.

Note: This recipe also works well served on top of anything else that would taste good with peppermint—chocolate pie, brownies, cupcakes, and so on.

Mix-ins and Topping Ideas for Hot Cocoa Bar

A great idea for holiday entertaining is to have a hot chocolate bar. Include a great assortment of mix-ins and toppings—use your imagination. This would be a great way to enjoy the holidays and begin a new tradition. You could even make it a contest and include awards for the most original flavor, best looking mug, and so on.

Serve a couple of basic hot cocoa options like classic and peppermint. Keep the hot cocoa warm by using a hot beverage dispenser or a slow cooker. Then have the mix-ins placed in serving bowls with spoons. Family and guests can fill their mugs with cocoa and then add the mix-ins and toppings of their choice to "customize" their cocoa.

Mix-ins:

- butterscotch chips
- cinnamon candies
- creamy peanut butter
- Nutella
- crushed peppermint candies

- crushed candy canes such as strawberry, orange, or cherry flavored
- crushed toffee bits
- crushed Butterfinger

- ice cream in various flavors such as vanilla, mint, or caramel
- chocolate syrup
- caramel syrup
- chopped peanut butter cups

Stirring Sticks:

- mini straws
- candy canes

- chocolate-coated spoons

- cinnamon sticks

Toppings:

- variety of marshmallows
- crushed candy canes
- various flavored whipped creams
- chocolate shavings

- Reddi-wip— they have chocolate and vanilla flavored
- chopped peanuts, hazelnuts, pecans

- mini M&M's
- marshmallow creme
- sprinkles or colored crystals

Mix-ins and Topping Ideas for Hot Apple Cider Bar

Another great idea for holiday entertaining is to have a hot apple cider bar. Start off with one or two yummy hot apple ciders. Keep the cider warm by using a hot beverage dispenser or a slow cooker. Have the mix-ins placed in serving bowls with spoons. Family and guests can fill their mugs with hot cider and then add mix-ins and toppings of their choice to "customize" their hot cider.

Mix-ins:

- flavored syrups such as pumpkin spice, white chocolate, or crème caramel

- maple syrup

- dulce de leche

- cinnamon candies

- caramel or butterscotch ice cream topping

- butterscotch candies

- ice cream in various flavors such as dulce de leche, rum raisin, or butter pecan

- caramel candies

Stirring Sticks:

- cinnamon-flavored candy canes

- mini straws

- cinnamon sticks

Toppings:

- various flavored whipped creams such as caramel, brown sugar, or cinnamon

- Reddi-wip

- caramel or butterscotch ice cream topping

- thin apple slices

- orange slices

- lemon slices

- chopped nuts

- cinnamon

- nutmeg

Also by Laura Powell

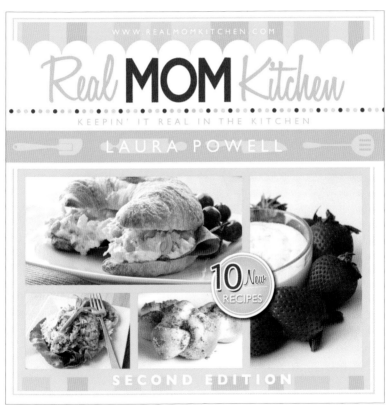

About the Author

Laura Powell grew up in the Salt Lake Valley. She gained a passion for cooking from her mother and created her own recipe book as a young girl in addition to participating in a summer cooking program through the *Deseret News*. She began her blog, realmomkitchen.com, in April 2008 as a way to showcase her passion for cooking. Since then, realmomkitchen.com has turned into her own small business. Laura continues to reside in Utah with her husband and three children.